First EADV International Spring Symposium

MALTA

27 February - 1 March 2003

With Compliments

EADV
MALTA

EADV

European Academy of
Dermatology & Venereology

MALTA
GOZO & COMINO
A TRAVEL PORTRAIT

PHOTOGRAPHY BY **JONATHAN BEACOM**

TEXT BY **GEOFFREY AQUILINA ROSS**

cover: The prow of a *Luzzu*, one of the islands' brightly-painted traditional fishing boats still in use today.

right: St Paul's Island where St Paul is said to have been shipwrecked in AD60.

page 4: The mediaeval walled city of Mdina sits at the centre of Malta commanding a view of the countryside.

page 6: As dawn breaks over Marsamxett Harbour the outline of the city of Valletta begins to take shape.

page 8: The islands' distinctive enclosed wooden balconies crowd together in St Paul's Street, Valletta.

page 10: The dramatic colours of dusk bring a mood of tranquillity to Rabat, Gozo, and to the Citadel that overlooks the town.

JONATHAN BEACOM: After working as a professional photographer with a London-based agency specializing in photo-interviews and, as a result, working with film and music celebrities on location in France, Spain and England, the Maltese photographer has turned his interests to travel photography. He has published a number of books including two on Malta that received international acclaim: *Malta - the hidden charms* and *The Maltese Islands from the air*.

GEOFFREY AQUILINA ROSS: journalist and writer. For many years a London magazine writer and a columnist on London's *Evening Standard*, he also edited a number of national magazines and was concept editor of *FHM*, one of today's most successful men's magazines. He has written a number of internationally published travel books and an amusing study, *How to Survive the Male Menopause*, that was translated into many languages.

The author and publishers have endeavored to ensure accuracy of all information in the book. However they can accept no responsibility for any loss, injury or inconvenience sustained by any traveller as a result of the information contained.

© Text: **Geoffrey Aquilina Ross**
© Photographs: **Jonathan Beacom**
Design: **Ramon Micallef**
Translations: **Intercom Translations**
www.intercom.translations.co.uk
Pre-press and printing: **Gutenberg Press Limited, Malta**

ISBN 99932-35-04-0

10 CONTENTS

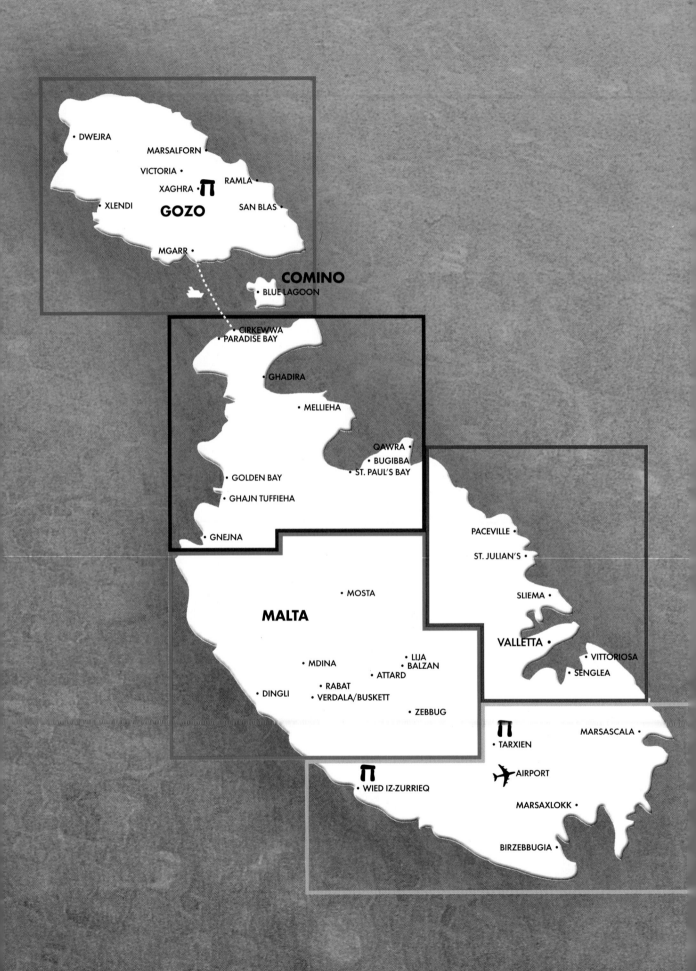

The Maltese archipelago is made up of three populated islands and a number of barren rocky outcrops that are home only to migratory birds and lizards. They sit at the crossroads of the Mediterranean, midway between Gibraltar and Port Said. Sicily lies to the north and the coastline of North Africa is to the south. The islands are tiny, sharing a total land area of little more than 400 sq km. Malta, the largest island, takes up 320 sq km, while the smallest, tiny Comino with a population of four permanent residents and one sporty hotel, is only about 13 sq km. There are no rivers or mountains, just low hills and fertile valleys, but these, together with the multitude of bays and inlets that make up the rocky coastline, give the islands considerable charm as well as a feeling of spaciousness.

Surrounded by clear blue sea, the islands have all the makings of a sunshine resort. But for anyone not content with lazing on the beach, there is a lot to see. The islands contain a considerable number of sites of great historical importance, many of them declared heritage sites by UNESCO. There are temples older than the pyramids and in the city of Valletta, the impressive capital edged by two great harbours, there are superb buildings like the Palace of the Grand Masters and St John's Co-Cathedral that were built by the knights of the Order of St John (who were later to become universally known as the Knights of Malta). Both contain unimaginable wealth and decorative distinction.

There is Mdina too, a mediaeval walled city, where descendants of ancient families still live close to their cathedral that rivals Valletta's in patrician houses handed down over the centuries. In Gozo, not only is there a superb megalithic temple, but dominating the countryside there is also a tiny citadel that in the late 16th century offered shelter to the island's inhabitants when corsairs raided the island in order to capture and sell them as slaves.

And everywhere you wander, bearing witness to the islanders' religious devotion, there are richly decorated baroque parish churches with painted ceilings and precious silver artifacts.

But in spite of the islands rich links with the past, modern life has not passed them by. There are excellent hotels and resorts, restaurants where the finest fresh fish is a speciality, and a way of life that is, for both the Maltese and the islands' visitors, relaxed.

The islands may be small, but there is more to them than first greets the eye. Everyone who explores is rewarded.

THE BIRTH OF MALTA

BC

5000-4000 Neolithic Age: The first settlers arrive, probably from the north.

4000-2500 The Temple Period: The unique megalithic temples of Hagar Qim and Mnajdra in Malta and Ggantija in Gozo are built. They are the oldest, free-standing stone edifices in the world.

2500-700 The Bronze Age: Settlers begin creating small villages.

700-550 Phoenician: Phoenician merchants trading in the Mediterranean make Malta their commercial centre.

550-218 Carthaginian: Carthaginians conquer Malta. The islands' strategic position now enables their ships to control the sea.

218-535 AD Roman: During Second Punic War, the Roman forces capture the islands. Malta is incorporated into Republic of Rome.

AD

60 St Paul is shipwrecked on his way for trial in Rome. Christianity is introduced to the Maltese.

117-138 During Hadrian's reign the islands are declared a Roman municipality.

395-500 Byzantine: Malta becomes part of the Eastern Roman Empire.

870-1127 Arab: Aghlabid Arabs invade from North Africa. They introduce Islam, their religion, and fruit like figs, citrus and pomegranate.

1127-1194 Norman: Count Roger II occupies Malta. He makes it part of Kingdom of Sicily.

1194-1266 Swabian (German): The Queen of Sicily marries the Duke of Swabia. The islands now fall under German rule.

1266-1282 Angevins (French): Charles of Anjou, brother of Louis IX, conquers the Kingdom of Naples and Sicily. The islands become part of his empire.

1282-1530 Aragonese (Spanish): Peter the Great, King of Aragon, helps the Sicilians massacre the Angevins. He takes over the islands.

1530-1798 Order of St John: The islands are given into the protection of the Order of St John of Jerusalem by Emperor Charles V of Spain. It is to be their new base from which to protect Christianity against Ottoman invasion.

1565	The Great Siege of Malta. On 18 May an armada of 181 ships carrying 30,000 fighting men descends on the Christian outpost. For three months Suleiman the Magnificent's force lays siege until help comes from Sicily. The Ottoman force flees, defeated.
1566	The city of Valletta is founded.
1798–1800	French: In 1789 Napoleon Bonaparte arrives with a fleet of 472 ships carrying 54,000 soldiers. Two days later the Grand Master surrenders the islands to the French without a shot being fired. The Order of St John is forced to depart, homeless.
1800–(1964)	British: The Maltese citizens rise against French occupation and seek allies to help rid them of their new masters. Britain offers help in the name of the King of the Two Sicilies. The French force is besieged in Valletta and capitulates. On 5 September 1800 the British flag flies over Valletta.
1814	Treaty of Paris awards Malta to Britain. The islands are officially a British Crown Colony.
1914-18	World War I. As the islands provide care for the wounded, Malta is known as Nurse of the Mediterranean.
1919	*Sette Giugno* riots. Post-war unemployment and poverty severely affect the islanders as the economy fails. Troops called in to control crowds in a Bread Riot shoot and kill four Maltese rioters.
1921	Self-government is granted by Britain. Malta's first parliament is convened.
1939-45	World War II.
1940	June 11. The first air raids come from Italy.
1942	Islands enter the Second Great Siege. More than 1,500 civilians are killed. Supply lines are cut and cause severe famine. People of Malta awarded George Cross for Gallantry by George VI.
1943	Italy surrenders. The Blockade of Malta ends and food supplies begin to arrive.
1964	Independence: Malta becomes independent state within British Commonwealth.
1974	Republic: Malta becomes a Republic with a ceremonial President within the Commonwealth.
1979	The last of the British force sails out of the Grand Harbour. After nearly 200 years the islands are no longer a British base.
1989	The Malta Summit: December 1–3. US President George Bush and Soviet leader Mikhail Gorbachev meet in Marsaxlokk Bay to mark end of Cold War.
1992	May 28–30. Queen Elizabeth II unveils Siege Bell during George Cross 50th anniversary celebrations.
1998	Malta submits second application for EU membership.
2001	Pope John Paul II visits for ceremony of beatification of three Maltese who gave their lives to religious devotion.

MALTA TODAY

The Republic of Malta maintains close ties with the trading partners of the European Union as well as countries as geographically distant as the United States and Japan. Foreign investment is welcomed, particularly in light industry, but it is tourism that accounts for the major portion of the national revenue.

More than one million tourists arrive each year and while many are looking for perfect sunshine holidays, a considerable percentage come to see the islands' important historical sites and enjoy the culture. The spread of excellent four and five-star hotels has encouraged prosperity. Politically the islands swing from left to right and back again with the elections, but in recent decades the islands have seen steady economic development and improving standards in health, education and housing. Poverty was eliminated long ago and at home the Maltese live in better comfort than ever before. Due to an antiquated public transport system, car ownership is increasing. Many families own more than one vehicle.

Schooling is compulsory up to the age of 16 and entries from government, church-run and private schools to the University of Malta are high. The islands remain Catholic although, in common with many European countries, church attendance is falling.

The famous Malta Dockyards, facing a competitive mar-

ket, are meeting today's challenges with a degree of success as they bid to repair and service some of the world's largest tankers, cruise liners and even warships while, in Marsaxlokk Bay, the Malta Freeport has expanded its duty-free distribution and shipment zone to meet the increasing demand for its services.

The tiny islands may have no resources except sea and sun but, none the less, they have already achieved as much as many a larger country with greater resources. Malta has come a long way since becoming a Republic and has the drive to go further.

THE PEOPLE

The Maltese nation reflects the many nationalities that have settled here over the centuries and many family names reflect their origins – particularly Italian, British and French. However, almost all would consider themselves to be truly Maltese.

The population is around 375,000 (of which 345,000 live in Malta) and it is thought that about the same number are resident abroad in countries like Australia, Britain and Canada where many families made their homes in the large scale emigration that followed World War II. The family and extended family is considered paramount and loyalty binds them together.

THE LANGUAGE

The two official languages are *Malti* (that is, Maltese) and English. Although in recent years English has become less spoken than it was, all officials, doctors and professionals speak English, Maltese and some Italian. Bus and taxi drivers may only speak Maltese.

Having accepted English as one of the national languages, the Maltese are now in a position to successfully teach it to students from all over Europe in English-as-a-foreign-language schools. *Malti* is a Semitic language, supposedly Phoenician in origin, although many words in daily use have been taken from English, French and Italian. The language is written in Roman characters so additional letters have been created to accommodate the pronunciation of Arabic sounding words when written. As a result the Maltese alphabet has 29 letters.

RELIGION

The Maltese are Catholic and the islands are generously dotted with churches and chapels, many of them centuries old. There are three cathedrals; two in Malta, one in Gozo. In addition to their religious role,

the interiors of most churches have points of interest.

The Malta cathedrals contain a wealth of treasure while most town and village churches are perfect examples of a local taste for lavish baroque decoration. All are at their finest during a *festa*, the weekend when their patron saint is honoured with band processions and fireworks. During a *festa* all the silver and fine damask drapery is on show. Visiting a church calls for 'decency' in dress as these splendid edifices are, above all, places of worship. Women should cover bare shoulders or deep plunging necklines. A scarf or shawl will do. Shorts worn by men as well as women may also cause problems.

MONEY MATTERS

Currency is the Maltese Lira (written as Lm) with each lira equal to 100 cents. There are notes to the value of Lm20, Lm10, Lm5 and Lm2. Coins are Lm1, 50c, 25c, 10c, 5c, 2c and 1c.

Visitors may bring any amount of money into Malta provided that if it is more than you might spend on holiday or business, the amount is declared on arrival. No more than Lm50 may be brought in. Visitors can take out any foreign currency that remains unspent and no more than Lm25.

CREDIT CARDS Most international charge cards are accepted in banks, ATM machines, shops, hotels and restaurants. However if you draw money at a bank counter you will need your passport or ID Card for identification.

MONEY CHANGE Best rates are available through banks and money exchanges who use official rates from the Central Bank of Malta.

BANKS There are branches of HSBC Bank, the Bank of Valletta, Lombard Bank and APS in major towns of Malta and Gozo. Banking hours change slightly in summer and winter depending on locality but usually are: Monday to Friday 0830-1230. Saturday 0800 - 1200.

FOOD AND DRINK

FOOD Cooking is Mediterranean in style with fresh produce available daily. Many restaurants are famed for their fresh fish. The kind of Maltese cooking you find in homes is, like Maltese bread, distinctive. It has a peasant simplicity and is influenced by Italy both in the cooking and availability of similar ingredients.

Today many restaurants pride themselves in offering Maltese favourites alongside more familiar international dishes. Although these may not be quite like Mamma would make, they do give an idea of what is enjoyed in Maltese homes. Maltese bread is truly delicious: crusty and full of flavour on its own, spread with butter or, Maltese style, as *hobz biz-zejt*. This is bread dribbled with oil, rubbed with halved tomatoes and sprinkled salt, pepper, fresh basil and sometimes capers. The Maltese are partial to *fenek*, that is rabbit, either fried or in a stew. And in September when *lampuki* (a dolphin fish – not to be mistaken for dolphin) are in season, they look forward to a pie made with fillets of fresh *lampuki*, tomatoes, cauliflower, spinach, onions, olives and parsley in a light pastry case. Other favourites worth trying are *timpana*, a macaroni pie made with minced meat, eggs and ricotta cheese set in a case of flaky pastry and, *gbejniet*, a cheese made from sheep or goat's milk that is enjoyed soft and fresh with a salad or allowed to harden and eaten with *galletti*, Malta's delightful plain crunchy biscuit.

DRINK Maltese wines have grown in popularity and quality, especially those from the three major wineries, Marsovin, Delicata and Meridiana. Beer has been brewed with great success locally for many decades and Cisk lager, Hop Leaf and Blue Label, all produced by the Farsons Brewery, match any beer brewed in Europe.

GETTING AROUND

BUS The bus service on the islands is being updated. Most of the bright yellow buses were at their newest in the 1950s and retain a certain charm if not comfort. Travel is inexpensive and slow with prices on most routes at 15 cents rising to a maximum of 40 cents on the longest routes. Tickets are usually purchased

from the driver. In Malta the central bus terminus is outside Valletta with buses setting out to all points of the island. Limited services also run from Sliema and Bugibba.

In Gozo the central terminus is in Victoria and the system operates in the same manner as Malta, but with fewer buses. All buses return to Victoria approximately 10 minutes after reaching their furthest destination. Gozo buses are painted grey with a single dark red stripe. Ferry passengers arriving in Gozo find the Victoria bus connection waiting on the quay.

It is always advisable to check the time of the last bus. Bus routes shut down early and there are few night buses.

BY CAR Many find driving on the islands a frightening experience. Driving is on the left but you must not expect any other rules or courtesies to be applied. Be prepared for slow cars in the outside lane while faster cars overtake on the inside, and cars pulling out onto main roads even if traffic is approaching at speed. Do not expect signals indicating when turning left or right. The speed limit is 40mph on highways; 25mph in towns and villages. Random breath-testing at night has been introduced in the hope of reducing alcohol-related accidents.

There are a large number of rental companies offering excellent modern cars in good condition. Charges vary, but all are rented with unlimited mileage. Rental drivers must be aged 25 or over and possess a valid driving licence. It is advisable to take out full insurance.

CHAUFFEUR Many companies have fleets of chauffeur-driven cars, usually shiny black Mercedes. These can be booked and used simply as taxis. If you need a cab late at night, use a chauffeur-driven car.

TAXIS are white and carry the recognised Taxi sign on the roof. They are all fitted with meters but many drivers refuse to use them. Always agree a price before entering a taxi. Taxis are only available from ranks and keep to their own hours of work.

The **KARROZZIN** The horse-drawn gharry, the charming *karrozzin*, has been in use since about 1850. For many years it was the only means of transport available but today the numbers have dwindled and the *karrozzin*, is used only for short sightseeing trips. Negotiate the price before setting off.

THE GREAT SIEGE
AND THE KNIGHTS OF MALTA

The arrival of the knights of the Order of St John of Jerusalem in 1530 changed the course of Malta's history. The knights brought with them a dedication to Catholicism that would endure and an incalculable wealth that would change the appearance of the islands and the lives of the inhabitants. Until their arrival the islanders were poor, the victims of plague and famine, living under permanent fear of invasion by the Ottoman Turks determined to advance with Islam onto Rome and Christian soil.

The Order of St John was established in 1048 in order to provide care for the poor and sick pilgrims visiting the Holy Sepulchre in Jerusalem. But by 1099, with the advent of the Crusades, the Order began to take on a military role as they fought to defend the religion.

Centuries later, as Islam continued to rise, the Ottoman Turks triumphed and the Order suffered many defeats. As they lost their bases so they moved on – to Acre, then to Cyprus and eventually to Rhodes where a final blow came on 1 January 1523. They were vanquished by the son of Suleiman the Magnificent, scourge of Christianity. and set sail, destination unknown. Seven years later, on 24 March 1530, Emperor Charles V in Spain, answered their prayers: he gave them Malta. The Knights recorded that the island was barren, difficult to defend and had 12,000 miserable inhabitants. But as they were homeless, they had little choice but to accept the offer.

THE GREAT SIEGE

In 1565 Suleiman, now past his 70th year, decided to again turn the might of his Ottoman force against his old enemy, the Order of St John. With an armada of 181 ships under Admiral Piali they sailed for Malta carrying more than 30,000 fighting men lead by General Mustapha Pasha. Joining them were the ships of the great corsair Dragut Rais.

To face them in Malta based around Fort St Angelo and what is today Senglea and Cospicua, Grand Master la Valette had about 600 knights and servants-at-arms, 1,200 infantrymen, mostly Italian and Spanish, and a Maltese militia of about 4,500 untrained men. In all (slaves included) the defenders totaled nearly 9,000.

On 18 May as the armada assembled off the coast of Malta presenting a sight no one would forget, all crops were quickly harvested and the water in the wells in the fields poisoned. The gates of the defensive positions were secured; the Order and the Maltese were as prepared as they could be.

The Turks besieged Fort St Elmo and for 31 days there was a barrage of fire as well as brutal land assaults. At one point the bodies of the dead lay so deep in the dry moat outside the Fort that they became bridges of decomposing flesh. When Mustapha Pasha ordered the heads of four decapitated Knights to be floated on shields across the harbour, the Grand Master ordered the heads of captured Turkish soldiers to be fired from mortars as cannon balls.

On 23 June Fort St Elmo fell. Only four Maltese survived the siege – by swimming across the harbour to Fort St Angelo. The Turks had lost 8,000 men.

The Turks then turned their fire on Fort St Angelo and the fortified community around it. The Order's stronghold presented an impregnable face from land and sea and during the hot summer each attack was repelled with conspicuous bravery and great cost to life until, on 7 September, a long-awaited relief force from the Viceroy of Sicily came to their rescue. 8,000 men put ashore near St Paul's Bay and the Turks, exhausted by the fighting and in no position to face well-fed soldiers fresh for battle, were routed. The siege was lifted. The Turks sailed home in disgrace having lost nearly 30,000 men. Of the 9,000 that made up Malta's defence force, just 600 remained.

Across Europe the crowned heads rejoiced as news of the victory spread and in gratitude began bestowing largesse upon the Order. Even the Protestant queen of England, Elizabeth I, sent a large sum of money. The Order became universally known as the Knights of Malta.

When the new city of Valletta was built it was named after Grand Master Jean Parisot de la Valette who lead the islands to victory.

VALLETTA - THE CITY CAPITAL

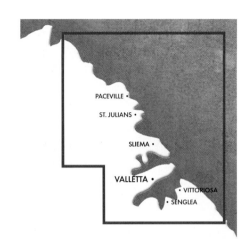

When Sir Walter Scott visited Valletta he wrote it was a 'city built by gentlemen for gentlemen' and it remains so even now, although much of its splendid architecture is concealed by the modern-day shopfronts.

On a narrow peninsula, with the Grand Harbour on one side and **Marsamxett Harbour** on the other, the city was built by the Knights in the triumphant years that came after victoriously defeating the Ottoman Turks in the Great Siege of 1565. **Fort St Elmo** stands guard at the entrance to the harbours and steep bastion walls wrap the fortified city.

One imposing palazzo is the **Auberge de Castille**, but venture further to discover the rich heritage contained within important buildings like the Palace of the Grand Masters and St John's Co-Cathedral.

1.9

In 1571, six years after the Great Siege, the Knights of the Order of St John set about creating a magisterial palace in their new city that would reflect the Grand Master's status. Architect Gerolamo Cassar who was already responsible for many of the city's fine palazzi was entrusted with the work and the Palace of the Grand Master took shape.

Today no visit to the city is complete without a tour of the Palace. The exterior is plain and gives little idea of the glorious interior, only long wooden **balconies** ornament its 89m façade. But enter through Neptune's Courtyard and ascend to the grand rooms above that are linked by long marble **corridors** with frescoed ceilings and paintings. See the Throne Room and State Dining Room as well as the **Red Room** that was the Grand Master's audience chamber and the **Tapestry Chamber** ornamented with impressive Gobelins tapestries (1697). The Armoury contains a fine collection from the days of the Knights.

VALLETTA - ST JOHN'S CO-CATHEDRAL

The austere exterior of St John's Co-Cathedral (begun in 1573) shows little sign of the remarkable splendour that lies within. It is only as you enter through the main door that you are overwhelmed by the Cathedral's magnificent decoration and colour. The floor is covered in 400 superb marble memorial slabs and the painted ceiling is a glorious spectacle by Mattia Preti (late 17C). To the side are tiny ornamented chapels while ahead is the richly embellished **High Altar** to complete the feast of opulence. In St John's Museum is **Caravaggio's** masterpiece *The Beheading of St John*.

The title Co-Cathedral means Conventual-cathedral: belonging to a religious brotherhood.

22

In the Museum are some of the most important archaeological treasures found on Malta and Gozo. Here, in a palazzo built as the Auberge de Provence by the Knights in 1575 and now being meticulously restored, are artifacts dating back to the pre-historic Temple Period, 4100-2500 BC, when the world's oldest free-standing stone edifices of Hagar Qim, Mnajdra and Ggantija were erected. Displays include jewelry, tools and pottery as well as carved stones used for decoration and the cult statues that once presided over the temples. Look for the **Sleeping Lady** statuettes and the **sarcophagus**.

23

The city, with its magnificent harbours on either side, is both an important historical site and thriving business centre. Not only are there a considerable number of places to see like museums, baroque churches and the early-18th century Manoel Theatre – as well as the more recent **Siege Bell Memorial** that honours the men who lost their lives in the wartime convoys of 1940-43 – but there are also bustling centres that bring the city to life. Like busy **Republic Square** with its shops and cafés and the crowded *Monti* street market where bargains can be found. For tranquillity there are the **Upper Barrakka** gardens with a spectacular view over the Grand Harbour.

25

IT'S CARNIVAL! For one long weekend in February, Valletta's main thoroughfares are taken over daily by a traditional carnival parade. On the four days preceding Ash Wednesday, the day on the religious calendar that heralds the beginning of Lent and a time for Catholics to fast, jollity takes to the streets. Bands parade, dance groups perform on the main squares and, bringing the spirit of fun closer to the crowds lining the streets, the parades include giant grotesque figures as well as clowns and cartoon characters recognised by every child. This is an unsophisticated event. Many children in the crowds dress up in costume too.

VALLETTA

THE THREE CITIES
SENGLEA, COSPICUA AND VITTORIOSA

Valletta, with its fortress and breakwater facing out to sea, lies between Marsamxett Harbour and the Grand Harbour. Residential Sliema is on the distant shore of Marsamxett while on the southern side of the Grand Harbour are the Three Cities of Senglea, Cospicua and Vittoriosa as well as a light-industry zone and the bustling dockyard that for centuries has been the focus of Malta's fame.

The Grand Harbour's deep, sheltered creeks on the south shore have been coveted by other nations since Phoenician traders began using the harbour as a commercial trading post between 700 - 550 BC. In fact, so strategically important did this harbour become that it often brought the islands into periods of conflict, the most recent being during World War II when Malta was considered vital to the success of the Allies campaigns in North Africa and southern Europe. Allied shipping sheltered, refueled and repaired here and as a result the harbour and this region received the heaviest aerial bombing ever recorded. In that conflict **Fort St Angelo** having long ago been the fortress of the Knights became the headquarters of the Royal Navy.

Today the Grand Harbour remains equally important but now its interests are purely commercial. Each day it welcomes some of the world's finest cruise ships as they bring their passengers ashore to tour the islands as well as the ferries that ply traffic and goods across the Mediterranean. The Dockyards, facing world competition, repair giant tankers and refurbish liners.

The Knights were based in the towns that are now Senglea, Cospicua and Vittoriosa until Valletta was built. In 1798, however, during the two-year French reign after the Knights had been despatched, the towns were given honorific titles of City by Napoleon's commander in the hope of getting the residents to submit to new French laws. The bribe did not succeed, but the honorary titles continue.

Regrettably many fine buildings were destroyed in World War II, but life has never slowed and new projects are bringing wealth back to the towns. While **Fort St Angelo** sometimes acts as the backdrop for a national *dghajsa* regatta and **Senglea**, wrapped in steep bastion walls draws visitors, development on the **Vittoriosa** waterfront will mean large yachts can moor on the marina close to the Maritime Museum and casino.

33

SENGLEA

SLIEMA
THE RESORT TOWN

Malta's prime residential area has flourished continuously since being established in the late-19th century as a relaxed seaside town where families could spend the hot summer months. It is now a popular resort that warmly welcomes tourists.

There are a variety of excellent hotels, restaurants and cafés as well as expensive new apartment buildings with sea views, language schools and quality shops. Cruise boats set out daily from the **Marsamxett Harbour** waterfront, but follow the coastal promenade that skirts the town and you come to many popular places where families enjoy swimming from the smooth cream-coloured rock shoreline.

37

SLIEMA PROMENADE

Sliema residents take great pride in the sweeping **promenade** that runs above the shoreline all the way to the St Julians district with its five-star hotels and splendid choice of restaurants and cafés. In the hot months there is nothing locals enjoy more than a leisurely stroll in the cool of the evening along its length, meeting friends and exchanging news. In the winter the sea may sometimes break over this coastline but in the long months of summer this ribbon of white rock is where families gather to swim in sea that is both clean and clear. **Independence Garden**, between the sea and promenade, is an oasis of calm.

ST JULIANS – LATE NIGHT VENUE

Fishermen may still bring their daily catches into this picturesque creek where ducks and cats live in harmony on the Spinola Bay waterfront, but with its wide selection of open-air restaurants and cafés, St. Julians is now better known for being a centre for good-eating and late nights.

Adjoining St Julians are Paceville and St George's Bay with four and five-star hotels, discos, a casino and yet more restaurants, bars and cafés. Together they create a popular entertainment area where many late-night places stay open until the early hours.

ON THE ROAD TO **ST PAUL'S BAY**

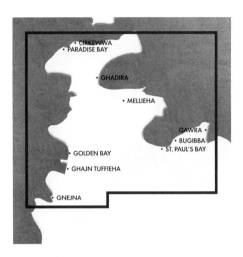

T he road leading northwards from the entertainments district of Paceville and St Julians suddenly opens up into sweeping vistas of a seemingly endless sun-bleached rocky coastline as it heads towards Bugibba, St Paul's Bay and the sandy beaches of Golden Bay, Ghajn Tuffieha and Ghadira before proceeding towards the Gozo ferry quay at Cirkewwa. This is a region that seems designed for holidays.

Along the coast are a number of small bays and rocky inlets popular with families for picnics and for swimmers who enjoy snorkeling. Many inlets are known only to locals who guard their secrecy but, by and large, where you see the Maltese swimming, it is an ideal place to swim. Visitors are welcome.

43

44

ST PAUL'S BAY – THE SHIPWRECK OF ST PAUL

Religious tradition says that St Paul was shipwrecked on Malta in AD 60 on his way to stand trial in Rome. The ship on which he was being transported ran aground in a storm, and local fishermen rushing to the rescue took the bedraggled survivors ashore where they lit a bonfire to help them get warm and dry. As St Paul picked up a branch to throw it onto the fire, a deadly snake bit him on the hand but, to everyone's astonishment, he shook it off and suffered no ill effects. It was, they all knew, a miracle and from that day the islands' indigenous snakes have been non-poisonous.

St Paul stayed in Malta for a short time, preaching, converting and baptising the first Maltese Christians. He remains one of Malta's most venerated saints and a number of churches and chapels have been built on sites said to have connections with him.

St Paul's Island jutting out on the northern side of the bay is where St Paul's ship is believed to have floundered. A statue was erected to the saint in 1845 and many day-cruise boats now call in at the island to give trippers a photo-opportunity. Seen only by divers or by passengers in a glass-bottomed cruise boat is a statue of Christ dropped off the island with the blessings of Pope Paul II in 1990.

BUGIBBA
DESIGNED FOR A HOLIDAY

From being a quiet little seaside community with a fine view across St Paul's Bay catering for just a modest number of visitors in the height of summer, Bugibba has transformed itself into a bustling holiday destination that flourishes most of the year. Life is centered around **Bay Square** and the wide selection of modern hotels with open air pools and lidos. There are all manner of inexpensive restaurants and cafés and from a jetty on the **Promenade** boat cruises set out daily, some going to Comino's Blue Lagoon, others around Gozo.

48

SEA AND SUN – **ON GOLDEN SANDS**

As the seasons change, so the islands take on a variety of different appearances. In the long summer months the sandy stretch of Golden Bay is a haven for families and friends as they gather to laze in the sun or shelter under brightly coloured umbrellas and then swim in the clear waters.

But in the short winter months, a sense of tranquillity descends. So too, occasionally, do horses. This unspoiled region around Ghajn Tuffieha is popular with riders. Here they can enjoy outings over spectacular hillsides that have not changed in centuries. This is a countryside as natural as nature intended and, with the arrival of spring, so the landscape slowly turns into a colourful patchwork as myriads of wild flowers begin to blossom. This is terrain for walkers too.

THE BEACHES OF THE NORTHWEST

Seen from the air all three sandy beaches on the northwestern coast promise enchanting stretches of sand set in an impressive landscape. There is rugged **Ghajn Tuffieha** that is reached by a long sweep of steep steps, **Golden Bay** with its modern hotel complex, and simple **Gnejna Bay** with a tower overlooking its boathouses, all of them offering everything young families could want in the summer season.

Dividing the beaches are dramatic sheer clay slopes. Adventurous swimmers often settle at their base.

MELLIEHA AND GHADIRA – HILL TOWN AND BEACH

Overlooking **Mellieha Bay** and sprawling across the top of the hillside is the town of **Mellieha**, with its parish church dedicated to the Nativity of Our Lady. To one side is a children's favourite location, the film set of **Popeye's Village**, while below is **Ghadira**, Malta's largest and most popular sandy beach where everyone enjoys wading out in the shallow water 'for miles'. There are beach establishments, cafés and restaurants and in addition to umbrellas and sun-beds, visitors can rent sail boats, jet skis and canoes as well as view the world from above as they paraglide behind a speedboat. Alongside the beach is a Nature Reserve with a small lake where many species of birds take shelter as they migrate to and from Europe and North Africa.

MARFA RIDGE – NEXT STOP GOZO

From the sandy beach of Ghadira the road rises steeply to Marfa Ridge, the most northern part of Malta. It is here, from the quays at **Cirkewwa**, that ferries sail across the Gozo Channel to Gozo and Comino. The ridge has a charm of its own. The **Red Tower**, erected as St Agatha's Tower in 1649 in order to defend northern Malta, sits majestically on the hill top overlooking the bay, while along the ridge and facing the island of Comino are the small sand bays of Armier and Little Armier. In a sheltered position surrounded by rugged scenery close to the ferry quay and modern hotel complex is **Paradise Bay**, one of the islands' favourite beaches.

MDINA
MEDIAEVAL CITY

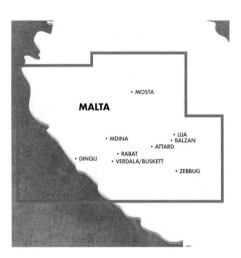

The mediaeval walled city that dominates the centre of the island was Malta's ancient capital. The Romans were the first to build on the site and successive conquerors lived there too. From this vantage point they could survey the countryside and, as its elevated position was easy to defend, be safe from attack. Within its walls were the islands' civic offices and the gracious houses where grand families lived in comfort close to the city's majestic cathedral.

The Knights strengthened Mdina's ramparts and bastion walls, but after Valletta was built at the end of the Great Siege of 1565, the new fortified city replaced it as the islands' capital. However Mdina has retained its architectural distinction and has superb places to visit.

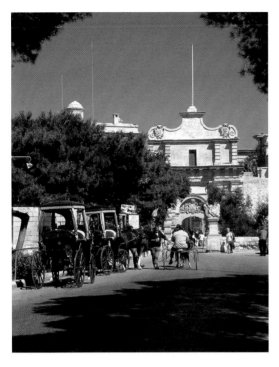

59

For many years Mdina was known as the Silent City; this was a mediaeval city of fine palazzi, monasteries and a superb cathedral but little more. Now, although only residents' cars may enter its walls, the advance of commercial interests has introduced restaurants, cafés and a five-star hotel. The city, however, remains an architectural gem and every street is worth exploring.

MDINA CATHEDRAL
DEDICATED TO ST PAUL

The Cathedral is believed to stand on the site of the house of Publius, St Paul's first Christian convert on the islands who later became the first Bishop of Malta. In 1693 a massive earthquake destroyed the original Siculo-Norman building and reconstruction started in 1697. It took five years to complete.

The exterior of the Cathedral gives little indication of the rich ornamentation that has been lavished within. It is only as visitors enter that the remarkable interior reveals itself. The ceiling is decorated with frescoes depicting *The Life of St Paul* (painted in 1794) and the floor is covered in slabs made of multi-coloured marble that commemorate leading Maltese ecclesiastics and prominent laymen. Ahead, adding to the inspired vista, is the decorative **High Altar** with its towering silver candlesticks and, on both sides, are delightful ornamented chapels. In the Chapel of the Annunciation by the High Altar is one of the Cathedral's treasures, a painting by the illustrious Mattia Preti. It depicts the miraculous appearance of St Paul to the citizens of Mdina during a Saracen raid in 1442.

THE CATHEDRAL MUSEUM
TREASURED BY THE CHURCH

The collections in the Museum are more historically important than they might first appear. Many are gifts to the church, others are items handed down through the country's religious foundations over the centuries. There are superb woodcuts by Durer and engravings by Goya among the paintings, drawings and engravings and among the many valuable documents are the archives of the Inquisition that ruled in Malta from 1574 until Napoleon abolished the office in 1798. (Of the 63 Inquisitors that served in Malta, two became Pope and 25 became cardinals.)

Many works on display graced Mdina Cathedral before earthquake devastation in 1693. These include Spanish painted panels showing the Life of St Paul (late-14C) and Virgin at Prayer by Sassoferrato (donated in 1687). A portable altar decorated with Byzantine enamel is believed to have been used in the galleys of the Order of St John. The building itself is impressive and also a curiosity because although its style is decorative baroque, it was built in 1733 as a seminary for an unostentatious, contemplative religious order. On one wall a plaque dated AD 679 states that the building stands on the site of the villa of Marcus Tullius Aristotle who lived there around 80BC.

TIMES GONE BY
PAGEANT OF THE KNIGHTS

Mdina's elegant streets often come alive with historical accuracy when triumphal pageants are presented and the thoroughfares suddenly look as they must have done in the day of the Knights. Soldiers in uniform lead the parades and the Grand Master and his noble Knights process from the Main Gate through the mediaeval city. Among the crowds lining the streets are townsfolk dressed in the costumes of the period. It is a wonderful way to see the streets of Mdina as once they were.

RABAT COMMERCIAL TOWN WITH ANCIENT ROOTS

The gracious baroque church dedicated to St Paul sits at the commercial centre of the old town surrounded by narrow winding streets and alleyways. With foundations dating from before 1692 when the dome was added, above its **high altar** is *The Shipwreck of St Paul*, a splendid painting by Stefano Erardi (1683) showing St Paul shaking off the viper that bit him after being shipwrecked. It is believed St Paul lived for some time in austere simplicity in the **grotto** beneath the church and even now with its statue of the saint (1748) presiding, the grotto is venerated and its stone credited with miraculous healing powers. Nearby are a number of eerie catacombs dug out between late 2C and early 4C. More than 1000 people were buried in **St Paul's Catacombs**. Facing Mdina, are the remains of a **Roman Villa** that was the home of a wealthy family.

VERDALA CASTLE
GRAND MASTER'S SUMMER RESIDENCE

Just outside Rabat on a road to Dingli Cliffs, Verdala Castle perches above Buskett Gardens in an enchanting woodland setting of citrus, cypress and pine trees. Designed by Girolamo Cassar in 1586 to look like a fortified keep, the castle was an agreeable summer palace for Grand Master Hugues Loubenx de Verdalle, a cardinal who revelled in the comforts of life. Friends were invited to hunt in the woods below as this countryside, at that time, was abundant with wild boar and wildlife. The Castle is now the President's summer residence but Buskett Gardens are open daily throughout the year, entrance free. On 29 June, the feast of St Peter and St Paul, it is the tradition for families to gather there for a picnic with food, wine and folk singing.

DINGLI CLIFFS
THE WEST COAST

The unsophisticated village of Dingli dominated by its baroque parish church sits in a rural landscape where time appears to stand still. Life seems to move at a farmer's pace and all through the year the fields seem abundant with crops. The village is close to Dingli Cliffs on Malta's western edge where the dramatic coastline is made up of a continuous line of sheer cliffs towering over the deep blue sea below. With most cliffs at around 250m, this is Malta's highest region.

In the cooler months this unspoiled countryside with its superb panoramic vistas becomes a favourite place for walkers who enjoy exploring the unique natural setting. In the Spring wild flowers add a wonderful tapestry of colour.

MOSTA
DOME OF DISTINCTION

The parish Church of the Assumption is unmistakable, and its superbly proportioned dome is visible from almost any vantage point on the island. In fact the Dome pinpoints the location of Mosta. But although the church is known generally as Mosta Dome, Mosta's parishioners prefer to refer to it by the name of the patron saint to whom it is dedicated: Santa Marija. The church is reputed to have the fourth largest unsupported dome in Europe – after the domes of St Peter's in Rome, St Paul's in London, and, believe it or not, a young rival at Xewkija in Gozo which was built to outshine Mosta in the 1950s.

The church was begun in 1833 when Mosta was still a village but the project was plagued with a series of misfortunes and took 28 years to complete. Its remarkable dome was constructed without scaffolding because it was built over and around a church already standing there. When it was completed the archbishop refused to bless it. The church is round rather than in the traditional Catholic shape of a crucifix so he claimed it was shaped like a mosque. A deputy was despatched to carry out the blessings.

In the sacristy is a bomb dropped during a Luftwaffe raid on 9 April 1942. It pierced the dome but miraculously did not explode. The congregation of more than 300 worshipers sheltering in the church, fled.

SAN ANTON GARDEN
THE GARDENS AT THE PRESIDENT'S PALACE

The President of Malta's official residence is San Anton Palace on the boundary of the villages of Balzan and Attard. Like many imposing houses it was initially a simple summer residence but in 1620, when Grand Master de Paule decided that travelling from Valletta to Verdala Castle was too far to contemplate, work was begun turning it into a palace.

Successive Grand Masters continued the tradition of adding to the imposing building, as did the British Governors and Maltese Presidents who would later take up residence. Today it is a gracious, elegantly proportioned palace with both public and private gardens. The Palace is only open to visitors for charity events but the public gardens are a favourite place for families to gather and for young children to feed the ducks and swans in the ponds. There are few flowers, just trees from all corners of the world.

THE THREE VILLAGES
ATTARD, BALZAN AND LIJA

The Three Villages of Attard, Balzan and Lija have grown to form one group and it is said that only local councilors now know where each village boundary lies. But each village has its own distinctive character and its own imposing parish church around which the village has grown.

The Church of the Assumption in Attard with its six niches on its façade honouring saints dates back to 1600 while Balzan's charming Church of the Annunciation was begun later, in 1669. All three villages have distinguished family palazzi and buildings that reflect traditional Maltese architecture.

HAGAR QIM

THE MEGALITHIC TEMPLES – OLDER THAN THE PYRAMIDS

Around 4100 BC the islands entered the era known as the Temple Period. At that time the islands formed part of a land mass across what is now the Mediterranean Sea and settlers began arriving from the north. They had no written language and their only tools were stone axes and flint. To move heavy rocks or boulders, they used wood or antlers as levers. Yet with these simple implements they constructed three of the oldest free-standing stone edifices in the world today.

Carbon dating suggests the first of these unique megalithic temples was Ggantija in Gozo, dated 3600 BC, but soon after came **Hagar Qim** and **Mnajdra** on Malta's western coastline overlooking the sea and the rock-island of Filfla.

MNAJDRA

THE MEGALITHIC TEMPLES

All three of the islands' unique temples are similar, outlined by massive stones the builders moved into position by rolling on stones shaped like cannon balls. Inside each temple there are clusters of rounded chambers with alcoves, altars and libation holes where wine or another liquid would have been poured in honour of a god. Holes cut high in doorways seem to indicate that wooden bars held curtains.

It is believed the temples were used for religious rituals linked to birth, death and rebirth. Carvings on many stones and many artifacts found in the temples show that animals were sacrificed to the gods and that cooked flesh was often offered to the congregation. Many of the 'fat figures' found at Hagar Qim are now on show at the Museum of Archaeology, Valletta.

WIED IZ-ZURRIEQ
AND THE BLUE GROTTO

On the coast outside the village of Zurrieq and just a short distance from Hagar Qim and Mnajdra temples is Wied iz-Zurrieq, a narrow fjord-like creek in the rocky coastline that has been used by fishermen as a shelter for many centuries.

It is a picturesque spot with just a few tiny dwellings and boathouses. Simple cafés have opened to cater for visitors to the area and many small boats cluster on the quay ready to take trippers to caverns along the coast to see the enchanting Blue Grotto that nature has created within the rugged coastline.

MARSAXLOKK BAY
HARBOUR FOR TRADITIONAL FISHING BOATS

Marsaxlokk Bay is deep and wide, a natural safe harbour where for centuries fishermen have landed their catches daily and kept their boats. Although the Malta Freeport has brought major shipping into the bay, the waterside village of Marsaxlokk remains a picturesque setting where little has changed over the years. Every Sunday a small fish market on the quay draws crowds looking for their seasonal favourites.

Large, modern fishing boats moor here too but it is the variety of brightly painted Maltese fishing boats, the *luzzu*, that gives this bay its remarkable colour and distinctive charm. On the waterfront where fishermen repair their nets are cafés and restaurants as well as an open-air market offering souvenirs to tourists. On 7 April, the feast day of St Gregory, crowds descend onto this waterfront for a traditional family outing, the first one of the year.

Catches of fish are landed almost daily throughout the year on Marsaxlokk's waterfront close to the parish church. Only fiercely rough seas during the winter months prevent the boats leaving harbour. As in many countries, fishing has become a family business with each member playing a role: from catching the fish at sea to selling it in the market. In this community, in search of tranquillity, some men even take the dog on a day's fishing trip.

TARXIEN AND THE HYPOGEUM
TEMPLES ABOVE AND BELOW GROUND

The bustling town of Paola conceals two more of the islands' ancient sites.

Forming a complex of three main temples surrounded by neolithic remains are the **Tarxien Temples** built in the last years of the Temple Builders era and only discovered in 1914 after farmers complained of huge stones in the rich soil damaging their ploughs. Many well preserved items found here are now in the Archaeology museum in Valletta but excellent copies illustrate how archaeologically important the site is. The **Hypogeum** is a unique underground labyrinth of rooms and burial chambers cut deep into the soft rock. More than 7,000 people were buried in the chambers. Visitors are limited to groups of no more than 10 at a time and only admitted with advance booking: telephone 21 825 579.

COMINO
ROMANTIC
AND RUGGED

DWEJRA •
MARSALFORN •
VICTORIA •
XAGHRA • RAMLA
XLENDI • GOZO SAN BLAS •
MGARR •
COMINO • BLUE LAGOON

The islands of Gozo and Comino lie to the north of Malta. Gozo, the second largest of the Maltese islands, is linked to Malta by a car ferry service sailing from Cirkewwa. Tiny Comino, with only a hotel and four permanent residents, is serviced by tiny passenger-only boats.

Comino Is little more than a picturesque rock. There are no roads just footpaths, and watching over the Gozo Channel there is St Mary's Tower. Today, instead of guarding against the corsairs and pirates from the Barbary Coast who used to shelter in these waters waiting for rich merchant ships to sail by, the tower sees nothing more menacing than pleasure craft heading for the Blue Lagoon.

87

The **Blue Lagoon** beckons. It is an enchanted spot with crystal clear water where even the youngest swimmers can feel safe in its sandy shallows. In the summer months the lagoon may seem crowded with boats but the tiny island also has two popular sheltered bays: **Santa Marija** and **San Niklaw**. The appeal of Comino is romantic, a wonderful place to escape to. But for anyone who wants action the island is perfect for watersports too, especially windsurfing, snorkelling and scuba diving. Sailing regattas often circle the island.

GOZO – ASHORE AT MGARR

For most visitors to Gozo their first step ashore is here, from the ferry link to Malta. It is at the port of Mgarr that they begin to appreciate that life in rural Gozo is different to the bustling pace of Malta. Life in Gozo is leisurely.

Mgarr is a pretty, working harbour with a small fishing fleet and a well-serviced yacht marina behind its two breakwaters. Overlooking the tiny bay where old boathouses have been transformed into excellent fish restaurants, is a pinnacled neo-Gothic church built in the late 19th C. On the land side are modern four and five-star hotels. Buses linked to the ferry arrivals and departures run from the quay to Victoria, the capital of Gozo.

THE FERTILE FIELDS – PROTECTED BY A CITADEL

The island of Gozo may be small but its countryside with low hills creates a feeling of spaciousness, especially when the terraced fields and hillsides turn into a patchwork of green ornamented with the colours of wild flowers and thyme. Even in sunbaked summer months many fields are abundant with seasonal produce: from lettuce and tomatoes to pumpkins and melons.

At the centre of the island is the charming town of **Victoria**, the capital, where life revolves around its central square, It-Tokk, with its open-air market and cafés. Many locals often call Victoria by its original name of Rabat. It was changed to Victoria in 1887 to commemorate the British queen's Diamond Jubilee.

On the hill rising above the town is the castle-like **Citadel** – known often as Il-Kastell or Cittadella. A Roman town once stood here and by mid-13thC a small Christian town had formed with small houses, hospital and chapel. In 1551 corsairs raided the island and carried off most of the population so a law was enacted ordering all Gozo's population to sleep within the Citadel. The law was only repealed in 1637 when the Knights were in control of the seas around Malta and Gozo. Today the walls surround the remains of mediaeval houses, some small local museums and a charming Cathedral designed, but on a much smaller scale, by Lorenzo Gafa who designed St John's Cathedral in Malta. It has no dome, but in 1739 Antonio Manuele di Messina painted a wonderful *trompe l-oeil* substitute that looks better when viewed from the interior than a real one could.

DWEJRA – THE INLAND SEA AND AZURE WINDOW

Gozo's landscape is often dramatic and perhaps the most spectacular view of all is at Dwejra near the village of San Lawrenz where the steep road drops sharply down to the sea.

Jutting out from the land, close to a dive site favoured by scuba divers, is the **Azure Window**, a massive, natural stone archway while, behind it, is the small but bewitching **Inland Sea** with its simple boathouses and cafés. From its tiny jetty boats take visitors though a narrow entrance to the deep sea outside. A short distance away is a watchtower built in 1651 and, in the bay, is **Fungus Rock** where a medicinal fungus treasured by the Knights was once said to grow.

TA' PINU
SANCTUARY
AND SHRINE

In 1883 a peasant woman heard the voice of the Virgin Mary telling her to pray in a small chapel in the fields nearby. A friend said he too had heard the voice and later the two prayed there for his mother who lay dying. She was miraculously cured and, as word spread, so people flocked to the chapel to pray and seek help.

By the 1920s the number had so increased that it was decided to build a new church to accommodate them and the neo-Romanesque Church of Ta'Pinu was created with the original chapel of miracles taking its place as a shrine behind the main altar. In a narrow corridor are naive votive paintings of people in peril and poignant relics of the search for a miracle. On the hillside is a recent Way of the Cross.

THE RUGGED COAST OF GOZO
THEATRICAL SPLENDOUR

The coastline to the south and west is both rugged and dramatic with sheer cliffs edging the deep sea below. Each vista is a superb sight that seems to change its outline as the sun rises and sets.

The watchtower at the tip of Xlendi bay casts a romantic illusion at sunset that, in the daylight hours, is replaced by one of superb drama similar to that of the long fjord-like inlet of Mgarr ix-Xini. These cliffs are a walkers paradise, especially near Sannat and Ta'Cenc in the spring months when they are covered in wild flowers.

MARSALFORN
SUMMER PLAYGROUND

The road from Victoria to Marsalforn Bay crosses fertile fields and passes low conical hills, one of which dominates the countryside with its figure of Christ the Saviour. **This statue is made of fibreglass as the original was damaged when struck by lightning.**

Once a simple fishing village, Marsalforn has grown into a relaxed resort with hotels, apartments, cafés and a wide selection of restaurants. The original harbour still shelters fishing boats, however, and fresh fish is landed daily. For swimmers there is a small shingle beach or a popular stretch of smooth white rock. Along the coast are salt pans that have been drying sea salt since Roman times.

XLENDI
RESORT IN MINIATURE

The smaller of the island's two resorts, Xlendi has great charm. It sits in a tiny, narrow bay protected by steep cliffs and has a slim strip of sand edging a waterfront planted with tamarisk trees along which is an elegant four-star hotel and cafés. Brightly coloured fishing boats anchor in the water.

On one side, the sheer cliff face has steps leading to Carolina's Cave where many years ago nuns would swim in privacy. On the other side, below holiday homes and apartments, a walkway popular with swimmers leads out towards the open sea. On the headland is a Knights' watchtower built in 1658.

SANDY BEACHES
SAN BLAS AND RAMLA

The island's two sandy beaches are on the northern coastline reached on winding roads leading down through fertile valleys from the sprawling hilltop village of Nadur.

Ramla, the larger of the two, is Gozo's most popular beach. In the winter months tranquillity descends, but in the hot months of summer cars park along the road just off the sand and simple cafés provide for the families who enjoy spending the whole day there. Above the red sand on the hillside is Calypso's Cave where according to local lore the fair nymph Calypso (referred to in Homer's *Odyssey*) kept Odysseus captive.

San Blas is much smaller, and much prettier. However it has no facilities because the only access to the beach is down a steep, narrow footpath through lemon groves and fig trees. It is a difficult climb and for only the very fit.

EXPLORING GOZO – FROM MEGALITHIC TEMPLE TO HOLIDAY HOME

The island of Gozo – known as *Ghawdex* by both the Maltese and the Gozitans – has a wonderful and surprising charm. And it is full of surprises too. For example, outside the village of Xaghra is **Ggantija**, the oldest of the Maltese megalithic temples, while **Xewkija** has the Rotunda church said to be the third largest unsupported dome in Europe. The villages all exert a lazy picturesque charm: there are cannons in **Zebbug**'s square by the parish church while **Xaghra** has an open-air restaurant to face its church. In and around the countryside are well-appointed farmhouses to rent, many with pools and fine views.

FESTAS & PROCESSIONS
RELIGIOUS CELEBRATION

Like most Catholic countries, the islands celebrate the holy days and saints' feast days on the religious calendar with a mixture of religious observance, pride and pleasure. Easter may be a solemn occasion when religious vows are renewed, but saints' days (known locally as *festas*) call for celebration.

Easter observance is a matter for solemnity and many villages on both islands have traditional, hours-long processions where heavy tableaux of life-size statues depicting scenes from the Way of the Cross are carried through the streets from the parish church by men garbed in white robes. Between each of the tableaux villagers dressed as people of the period, from Roman soldiers to simple shepherds, form part of the procession. Often faithful members of the congregation follow too making a personal pilgrimage.

A *festa*, however, is a spirited, joyous event in the summer months when the village patron saint's statue is noisily paraded through the parish streets accompanied by brass bands and their supporters, church bells and loud petards that blast the sky above to make it seem as if war has been declared. Everyone in the crowd thronging to watch the procession wears their finest clothes as they listen to the music and eat fast food or local nougat from the stalls that have set up in the village square. What they like best of all are the latenight massive fireworks displays without which no parish *festa* would be complete.

HIDDEN CHARMS IMAGES OF THE ISLANDS

One of the pleasures of the islands is exploring the countryside and the villages with their winding streets and alleys. Although the islands have embraced modern life there are still corners that retain a natural Maltese charm, corners where life seems a leisurely contrast to the modern commercial life in the towns and resort areas with their grand hotels, apartment blocks and busy nightlife.

Religion plays an important part in family life and has done so for many centuries – as the wayside chapels, statues and little niches in many streets prove. So do many small bars where sweet hot coffee or tea in a glass is served from early morning until workers and farmers return home after a day's toil. The soft limestone used for building gives the Maltese architecture its distinctive appearance, as do the enclosed wooden balconies. Add brightly coloured paint to these and you have a charm that is uniquely Maltese.

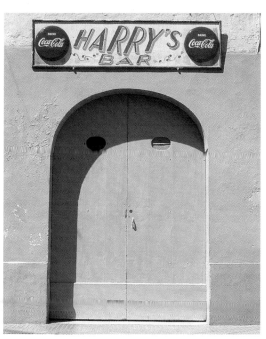

ACKNOWLEDGMENT

The publisher would like to thank the many people of Malta, Gozo and Comino who contributed to the making of this book. Thanks are due also to the Malta Tourism Authority.

All photographs by Jonathan Beacom except:
p.22 (bottom) and p.23 (bottom left) – Malta Tourism Authority;
p.65 (bottom left) and p.84 (bottom) – Kevin Casha.